AF893550

This Book Belongs To

Julie and Tom reached their elementary school - 'St Mark Elementary School'. They were here to interview their second grade teacher Ms. Rose Smith, for their class assignment. They were interviewing different professionals and trying to find more about their profession.

They were happy that they had reached the school on time and they saw Ms Rose Smith climbing up the steps to the school.

"Good Morning Ms. Rose!" they wished in chorus. Ms Smith smiled back and said, "Good morning darlings!"

Without further ado, Tom pops his first question, "Ms Smith, we'd like to know what a day in the life of a teacher is like."

Ms Smith smiled and said, "Well, it depends on the country, state, and also the grade we are teaching. There are teachers who teach kindergarten, elementary or primary level, middle school, high school, university etc. Then again there are specialized teachers for languages, vocational learning and special education. For each level different set of qualifications and skills are required".

"We are more interested to know about your day", said Julie as they all stepped into the hallway.

"Ok. Since I teach elementary level, I will tell you about a day in the life of an elementary teacher. Follow me."

The hallway was in its usual state of chaos. Ms Smith looked around and smiled, "A typical day for a teacher begins with taking a roll call, making any important announcement, meeting any visitor or parents before starting with the lessons" said Ms Smith. "Sometimes there is just enough time to grab a cup of coffee."

"How is teaching elementary classes different from teaching any other class?" was Tom's next question.

"Well!" said Ms Smith, "Though each stage brings with it its own challenges, teaching five to ten year olds is most challenging. They not only need help in the smallest of things like tying their shoelaces or understanding concepts but also derive their greatest joy from equally little things like a bubble in the wind or a squirrel on the window ledge. They get distracted easily. So a teacher has to constantly try to create interesting, fun filled lessons and retain their interest."

"I remember that I was always excited about coming to school when I was in second grade because there was always a surprise waiting for us," said Julie.

"Yes, in an elementary class, the way you teach is as important as the content of what is being taught. As a teacher we have to keep in mind the various ways in which children learn."

Julie who was amazed at this and asked, "How can there be

different ways to learn? I always thought we all learn the same way!"

At this Ms Smith smiled and said, "Well! There are some children who like pictures, some like to listen to music and some learn through an activity. At elementary school, we try to incorporate all the methods of learning so that each child grasps and learns the way which is best suited for him or her."

12
9
6

"So that means a teacher has to be very creative," said Tom.

"More than being creative, an elementary school teacher needs to have very good social skills and be able to don many hats. An elementary teacher must be proficient in multiple disciplines." answered Ms. Smith."

"Many hats? How is that so, Ms Smith?" was Julie's query.

"Well! A teacher is not only an educator but she is also a mentor, guide, parent, nurse, coach, artist etc. Depending on the need of the hour she has to wipe a tear or two, amuse the class with funny anecdotes, listen to them like a parent and help them learn not only the lessons in the text but also lessons from everyday life."

"Wow! We never thought about it!" said Tom.

Just then the bell rang signaling the end of the class. As they walked towards the yard Tom asked, "Besides teaching in the class, what are the other duties of a teacher?"

"Well! Planning is a very important part of a teacher's life. We have to plan for daily lessons, there are weekly and monthly plans as well as year-long plans. You see the bus over there?" said Ms Smith pointing to a yellow school bus in the yard. "The fourth grade students are going for a visit to the Natural History Museum. Their teachers have planned not only which exhibits the students must see, but also the assignments and projects that would follow."

"Wow! For us any trip out of the school is a fun outing. We didn't know that it is a planned lesson!" quipped Julie.

"As teachers we also have to plan for extracurricular activities and other duties which are part of our job." added Ms Smith.

"Wow! And do you handle all this on your own?" asked Tom

"Some schools provide an assistant teacher. But most of the work is done by the teachers on their own." said Ms Smith

"You know Ms Smith, as kids we have always wondered where do teachers disappear when they are not taking a class."

Ms Smith laughed and said, "Sometimes we just relax in the staff room, or the common room. But many times we have to attend meetings. There are subject meetings, staff meetings, special meetings, and PTA meetings. There is one going on right now. Come I'll take you there."

Julie and Tom followed Ms Smith down the corridor to the staff room, and were thrilled to be there as it was out of bounds for the students. When the other teachers were informed about Julie and Toms assignment they also gave their inputs and shared their experiences.

Ms Grey their third grade teacher offered them some cookies, while Mr. Nelson quizzed them about their interviews of other professionals.

Just then the lunch bell rang and Ms Smith said, "Come lets go to the cafeteria and grab something to eat. You two must be famished." She then ushered them to the cafeteria.

Tom and Julie were feeling very special because they were sitting next to their favourite teacher in the cafeteria.

Julie asked "Ms Smith what do you do when the school is off?"

"As teachers we do get a break when the school is off, but this is also a time when all our planning is done. A teacher who loves her job will take pictures, which she can share with her students, she will visit stores for teaching materials

she can use in her class, she will collect information which her students will find interesting. We carry loads of work home, even for the holidays."

Julie was amazed. "We thought only students get holiday homework. We never liked them. But now I realize their importance.

As they walked back to Ms Smith's class, Tom asked "Don't you get tired Ms Smith?"

Ms Smith smiled, hugged Julie and Tom and said, "No. All said and done, even with the long hours and chaotic and unexpected days, when I look at my class, I see angelic faces smiling at me. I feel I am making a difference and that makes my day."

Finally, when the last bell rang Julie and Tom said goodbye to their favourite teacher and trudged back home.

Titles of This Series